D1276041

Meditations My Rebbe Taught Me
Book 1

THE BOOK
OF PURPOSE

Rabbi Tzvi Freeman

Published by Class One Press   ISBN 0-9682408-5-2
ClassOne@theRebbe.com

Printed in People's Republic of China

Cover Art: Cube of Fire, copyright 2001, Robert Barnes

By the same author:

- Bringing Heaven Down To Earth
  —365 meditations of the Rebbe

- Men, Women & Kabala
  —guidance from the masters

- Heaven Exposed

For more, visit theRebbe.com and Chabad.org

They asked the tzadik, Rabbi Menachem Mendel of Kotzk, "Why are we told to place holy words upon our heart? Why not inside our heart?"

"We can only place these words upon our heart," he answered. "But perhaps one day the heart will shake, a small fissure will open and the words will fall inside."

That's why I call these words meditations—because the last thing I want is for you to read this book through, put it down and say, "That was nice."
I want you to write these words on your heart.
I want you to meditate.

How do you meditate on words? You need to get past the words. You need to get to the life pulsating within them. Liberate that life. Perhaps it is your own.

Perhaps your life is a commentary on these words. Perhaps the words will liberate you.

This series of meditation books holds tightly packed nuggets of wisdom garnered from the teachings of "the Rebbe", Rabbi Menachem M. Schneerson. This first book dances around the idea of Purpose. But first, let me provide some context:

Purpose is the antithesis of despair.

Whatever despair will tell you, purpose will say the opposite. And if you want to understand purpose, listen to the person in despair and invert his words.

Personally, I don't know how it was that a human being came up with this idea, this notion that life has purpose. Who first managed to look at life from beyond life and see that it is was made to go somewhere? Perhaps it could only be through a Divine voice. Perhaps to Abraham. Perhaps it was known from the dawn of human consciousness, but then forgotten and rediscovered. Certainly it wasn't always popular. Even today, many who call themselves enlightened find it hard to accept.

But there is no idea as empowering and as vital. Without the idea of purpose, what is life other than a snare to escape? How would we measure the dignity of a human being if none of our lives had inherent worth? What would drive us to preserve our world and treasure its beauty if we believed that nothing is of lasting value?

So somehow the notion of purpose found its way into the human psyche: That just as the universe appears intelligent within space—with a oneness of design, an elegance of repeated patterns and symmetries, to the point that as scientists we are convinced there must be a single, unifying principle behind it all—so too in time: with a beginning, a middle and an ultimate goal. That at the core of all that exists lies not a placid stillness; not an indifferent, transcendent Being contemplating his navel; but a burning purpose—along with a boundless delight in seeing that purpose fulfilled. That every croak and buzz; every blade of grass, every planet, every rock and sub-atomic particle plays a unique part in achieving that purpose. And that it is a purpose in which each and every human being plays the leading role; because we are the radical factor, the being that chooses the notes we wish to play.

So the first book of meditations is the Book of Purpose, because this is a meditation that changes everything. Because, otherwise, you might contemplate deep ideas, open your eyes to wisdom and behold new depths—and do absolutely nothing about it. So we start by telling you, "Move! Do something!"

After all, if you don't move, how will the words ever fall inside your heart?

Some of these meditations, such as *Life in Words*, are almost direct translations. Others are paraphrases or interpretations. Some are from the Rebbe's predecessors. All of them appeared at some time or other in "A Daily Dose of Wisdom from the Rebbe," emailed out by Chabad.org. I've included some informal jottings about sources for most of them.

I wish to thank my precious wife, Nomi, for her insightful comments and edits, and for putting up with my temporary disappearance acts in the process of writing this work.

What is the purpose?

The One Above desires to dwell in things below. The transcendent within the mundane.

Meaning that a breath of G-dly life descends below and dresses itself in a body and human personality. And this body and personality come to negate and conceal the light of this G-dly soul...

And nevertheless, the soul purifies and elevates the body, the person and even her share of the world.

And what is the reason behind this purpose?

There is none.

It is from before reason.
And so it is unbounded and all-consuming.

For it is a desire of the Essence.

—from the Rebbe's discussions of his father-in-law's last discourse.

9

Do not be misled by those who claim
there is no purpose.
They may know life,
but not the bowels of its fountain.

They may know darkness, but not its meaning.

They may have wisdom, but they cannot reach higher,
to a place beyond wisdom
from which all wisdom began.

They may reach so high until the very source from
which all rivers flow. To the place where all known
things converge, where all knowledge is one.
But they have not touched the Essence.

At the Essence there is nothing—no light, no darkness,
no knowledge, no convergence, no wisdom—nothing
but the burning purpose of this moment now.

—as per the Purim maamar
edited for 1991

Before your soul descended to this world, it was determined she would succeed. If not in this lifetime, then in another, or yet another—eventually she will fulfill her entire mission. And in each lifetime, she will move further ahead.

It was this knowledge that conceived her.

It was this inspiration that brought the world to be.

It is this vision of her success
that lies at the essence of all things.

—from the Rebbe's talks after his heart attack in 1977

Why are you afraid? Why do you panic?

Your soul plunged downward to live in an earthly realm, to enwrap herself in a body of flesh and blood, willingly and with purpose.

What emboldened her? What drew her to squeeze into the straitjacket of time and space?

It was neither fear, nor dread, nor panic.
It was the knowledge that here below
is a beauty the highest of angels cannot touch.

Care for yourself, for your family, for your fellow
human beings and our lovely planet earth,
not out of fear, nor from distress,

but out of love and awe
for the beauty within
that we came to uncover.

When the Divine Light began its epic descent—a journey that conceived worlds lower and lower for endless worlds, condensing its unbounded state again and again into innumerable finite packages until focused to a fine, crystallized resolution—it did so with purpose: to bring forth a world of continuous ascent. Since that beginning, not a day has passed that does not transcend its yesterday.

Like a mighty river rushing to reach its ocean, no dam can hold it back, no creature can struggle against its current. Even we, its voyageurs, cannot turn back. We must only move on with the river, on in its relentless ascent to the sea.

We may appear to take a wrong turn, to lose a day in failure—it is our delusion, for we have no map to know the river's way. We see from within, but the river knows its path from Above. And to that place Above it is drawn.

We are not masters of that river— not of our ultimate destiny, not of the stops along the way, not even of the direction of our travel. We did not create the river—its flow creates us. It is the blood and soul of our world, its pulse and its very fibers.

Yet of one thing we have been granted mastery: Not of the journey, but of our role within it. How soon will we arrive? How complete? How fulfilled? Will we be the spectators? The props? Or will we be the heroes?

That is all. And that is all that counts.

—Likutei Sichos, vol. 5, page 65 (there's more. much more)

Ultimately, she finds there is something
even more momentous than herself.
There is her purpose.

To accomplish, to heal, to make better—these, she
discovers, take precedent over her very being.

And in that moment of discovery she graduates from
being G–d's little child
to become absorbed within the body of the King.

—from a printed talk

We were not placed here to do the possible. Let the heavenly beings bring cause into effect, potential into actual. He did not breathe from His innermost depths into flesh and blood to achieve the facile and the ordinary.

We are here to achieve the impossible: To teach the world tricks it thinks it cannot do. To bring into its boundaries that which it cannot contain. To make the blind see, the deaf hear, darkness shine. To make everyday business into mystic union. To rip away the façade of the world and cause it to confess its conspiracy with the Divine.

When they tell you, "You can't go there! It's beyond you!"—grab that path as your destiny.

—from a letter

The history of humankind is not about the rise and fall of empires, nor about their wars and conquests. It is about a different sort of battle, the battle of whether the Divine Presence belongs here below or in some heaven above.

Those who believe She belongs in Her heavens destroy the earth.

Those who believe She belongs on earth, they build heaven here on earth.

That is the battle each one of us fights, and that is the story of all humanity's journey.

It is all that really matters. For that is all there is to any human being.

You have to begin with the knowledge that there is nothing perfect in this world.

In fact, almost everything is a mess.

Our job is not to seek perfection and live within it.

It is to take whatever broken pieces we have found and sew them together as best we can.

—from a letter

There are no things.

There are only words.

The Divine Words of Creation.

The words become fragmented, their letters scattered. Only then are they called things; for scattered, they have no meaning. Words in exile.

If so, their redemption lies in the story we tell with them. Reorganizing stuff into meaning, things into words, redefining what is real and what is not, and living life accordingly.

Life is in the interpretation.

There are those who chase the infinite

—and find they cannot live.

There are those who chase all things finite.

Their life is not worth living.

Redemption is when the infinite is at home

within our finite world.

—from a talk, spring of '91 (Iyar 5751)

There are three things to always remember:

The One Above,
yourself below,
and the world in between.

Abandon any one of those
and you will stumble and fall.

Even those who grasp for G–d alone,
they do not build, but desolate.

To reach G–d, you must deal with
the reality of your world
and redeem it.

—from the same talk

Some would like to remain aloof as the sun, removed from all matters of this world. Any occupation they are forced to have with planet earth is little more than a nuisance—they have higher things in sight. They invest little and gain even less.

Others fetter their very souls in the chains of life, suffer its scars and bruises, delight in its offerings, thirst for its rewards and tremble at its horrors. They invest everything and risk losing all of it.

True tzadikim emulate their Creator. To them, every detail of life has meaning, every step is a decision, every move is deliberate. And yet, they remain above it all.

What is their secret? It is memory.

They remember they are not the body, but the soul.

Yesterday, you were inspired.

Today, that is all gone.

And so, you are depressed.

But this is the way the system works: Everything
begins with inspiration.

Then the inspiration steps aside

—to make room for you to do something with it.

For fire to become deeds.

—from a letter

Our souls are windows for the world to receive light, pores through which it breathes, channels to its supernal source. They are its lifeline.

When we do good, speak words of kindness and teach wisdom, those windows open wide.

When we fail, they cloud over and shut tight.

It is such a shame, this loss of light, this lost breath of fresh air. A stain can be washed away, but a moment of life, can it ever be returned?

—sometimes the meaning comes only after you've forgotten the source.

At the outset of Creation, He removed all light. And that is the source of all that ever goes wrong.

Why did He remove the light? Why did He choose that things could go wrong?

Sometimes we say He wanted darkness as a background, a place to shine a new light and make a world of light. The darkness, we say, is there for the sake of light. Pain exists for the sake of healing.

But this could not be the entire answer.

Why? Because darkness for the purpose of light is not complete darkness. This darkness at the beginning was absolute, a void, an emptiness, the antithesis of the Infinite Light that preceded it. And so, too, we find evil in the world that has no explanation, no answer, no light to shine. Infinitely Dark.

The entire answer must be that in Light alone, G–d cannot be found. For He is beyond dark and light, presence and absence, being and not being.

And so, just as darkness is there for the sake of light, so is light there for the sake of darkness—to reveal its true purpose, to allow knowledge of a wholly transcendent G–d to enter His world.

—from the maamar published for the previous Rebbe's 40th yartzeit

Free choice lies at G–d's essence, for He alone is a truly free agent. From His essence, He breathes into Man's nostrils and Man too becomes free to choose his destiny. And in that choice lies the Essence.

The darkness, the confusion, the possibility of evil then has a purpose of its own—and that is to be the stage for Man's free choice, to allow G–d's essence to enter.

And if a person would choose evil? Would G–d's essence then be revealed?

No. For just as light needs a darkness in which to shine, so darkness needs light to reveal it's true purpose. Only when the choice is to do good, then light comes and reveals the essential truth of the darkness.

—same maamar as above. A gotta-learn maamar.

There is you, there is everybody else
and then there is your child.

The child is not just another of everybody else.
The child is you.

Yet not you;
someone other than you.

The child is both—for the child is born of the Essence
that transcends you and other.

We are children of the Infinite Light.

We are empowered to make the otherness into light.

—mostly from the Rosh Hashana maamar, edited 5751

Everything in the universe works in a chain of cause and effect. At the beginning of every such chain lies a decision, a free choice for which there is no cause, nothing that forced it to be that way. Whatever comes out of that chain will come back to the one who initiated it.

At the beginning of each chain and at its end, there lies purpose.

—attributed to the previous Rebbe

There is no such thing as an easy decision. G–d put you on this earth to make choices and it's going to be hard.

In fact, to be a real choice, both paths must appear attractive. Only by choosing to look deeper can you find which path leads to life.

That is the free choice we have:

To look deeper and deeper each time.

—from a letter

I f all the world is a classroom and all of life is a lesson, then certainly your profession and workplace are included.

After all, He has unlimited ways to provide your livelihood —why did He direct you to this way of life?

What is here that awaits you?

—countless

If it is not evil, we must use it for good.
If it can be raised higher,
we cannot leave it in the dirt.

Everything He made, He made for His glory.

—same

The ego is not to be destroyed.

It, too, is a creation of G‑d
—and all that He made,
He made for His glory.

Only this: that the ego must know that it is a creation,
and that all He made, He made for His glory.

—talks on the concept of proxy in Torah, see especially LS
vol. 33, Korach 2

What does ego have to do with purpose?
Shouldn't this be in another book?

—because reframed within Purpose, Ego is disarmed.

33

We are representatives of Above. And as such, live two lives at once:

We are free-thinking, independent beings.

And we are no more than messengers of Above.

It is a play of opposites in a single being.
An impossibility realized in true-life drama.

Just the sort of thing the One Above delights in.
For He, too, is impossible.

—same

The sages said about arrogance, "Damned is the one who has it, and damned is the one who does not."

Arrogance makes a mortal being into an idol. But without it, how can we change the world?

Let your conscious mind know it is nothing, and the power G–d has placed in your heart may then burst forth.

—from a short maamar of the Alter Rebbe

G–d made the heart of David and his soldiers strong and brave, so they would win in battle against Israel's enemies.

He made the hearts of Rabbi Eliezer and Rabbi Akiva stubborn, so they could go from ignorance to enlightenment overnight.

They were all men who saw their own nothingness, who realized they were less than dust before the Infinite.

But the brazen courage, the stubbornness that G–d put in their hearts, that they would not surrender.

But is this not ego? How could they feel as nothing and be stubborn and brave at once?

No, it is not ego. It is the Infinite Itself.

—same

To achieve wonders takes a fearless heart and a humble mind.

True, courage and humility are two opposite directions for the soul to travel at once.

But they take place in two distinct chambers:

The mind awakens to its nothingness
and the heart G-d gave you is bared in all its power.

—same

There is a place within the heart that only G-d knows. It is not something of which you are aware, or can ever be aware. Yet for its sake you were formed.

It contains your purpose. It is that which G-d delights of in you. For your Creator, it is you.

All of you must become transparent, a nothingness. And this treasure can then shine forth.

—same

The ego is not a source of strength.

It is weakness in disguise.

Inside there is invincible strength.

Remove the cloud of the mind's ego, and the inner power will shine through.

> —a common theme
> echoing in my ears
> from the Rebbe's farbrengens

G–d wanted a being—a somebody—not a puppet. A creature that would decide, "This is how it should be done, using such-and-such and in such a way with such a feeling—this is what my Creator wants from me."

The score is handed to us, but the music comes from our own souls.

—again, the talks on proxy

Today you did some wonderful things.

It's okay to tell yourself that.

There's a time to feel some satisfaction with what you have accomplished today.

As long as you're never satisfied with tomorrow.

—heard from someone who received this reply from the Rebbe

Do good with all your ego.

Say, "*I* need to make this happen."

Say, "*I* have to see this done."

Not only is this "I" permissible, it is crucial to getting things done.

So what is forbidden?

To believe the "I" belongs to you.

—the proxy thing again

You need to take ownership of those things important in life—the charity you give, the kind deeds you do, the Torah you learn and teach. You can't just say, "This is G-d's business, He has to take care of it." It has to hurt when it doesn't work out; you have to dance with joy when it does.

That is why G-d created the "I"—so that we would do these things as owners, not as hired hands.

—again

Prayer, meditation, acts of kindness—those all fulfill *our* needs.

We need air, we need water, we need to stay connected with our Source above.

Your work, your family, your path in the world—those fulfill a Divine desire.

It is He that wishes to find a home in this world He has made.

—from a letter

In your worldly business, just do what needs to be done and trust in G–d to fill in the rest.

In your spiritual business, however, you'll have to take the whole thing on your own shoulders.

Don't rely on G–d to heal the sick, help the poor, educate the ignorant and teach you wisdom.

He's relying on you.

—Hayom Yom

This experience,

    to give life,

    to watch it grow,

to be torn apart by it,

to receive pleasure from it and to give life again

—for this the soul descended from its ethereal heights.

And when it shall return to there, enveloped in these
souvenirs, it will finally know their depth.

And with them travel ever higher and higher.

ot with toil and not with struggle, but by the word of His mouth did the One Above create His world.

Not with toil and not with struggle, but with words of wisdom and kindness does He require we sustain it.

If so, what is the effort He demands from us?

That we invest our very essence in those words, as He invested His very essence within this world He made.

view it here:
http://www.chabad.org/multimedia/livingtorah.asp?AID=130728#

This goal, when will we reach it?

It was once far, but now it is near.

When will we hold it in our hands?

*When we will open our eyes to see
it is already here.*

—among the last words we heard from the Rebbe